KARATE

NEIL MORRIS

Heinemann
LIBRARY

www.heinemann.co.uk
Visit our website to find out more information about **Heinemann Library** books.

To order:
☎ Phone 44 (0) 1865 888066
📄 Send a fax to 44 (0) 1865 314091
💻 Visit the Heinemann Bookshop at www.heinemann.co.uk/library to browse our catalogue and order online.

First published in Great Britain by Heinemann Library, Halley Court, Jordan Hill, Oxford OX2 8EJ, a division of Reed Educational and Professional Publishing Ltd. Heinemann is a registered trademark of Reed Educational & Professional Publishing Limited.

OXFORD MELBOURNE AUCKLAND JOHANNESBURG BLANTYRE
GABORONE IBADAN PORTSMOUTH NH (USA) CHICAGO

Designed by Ken Vail Graphic Design
Illustrations by Mike Lacey (Simon Girling & Associates)
Originated by Dot Gradations
Printed by Wing King Tong in Hong Kong.

ISBN 0 431 11042 5   796.8153
05 04 03 02 01
10 9 8 7 6 5 4 3 2 1

British Library Cataloguing in Publication Data

Morris, Neil, 1946–
   Karate. – (Get going! Martial arts)
   1. Karate – Juvenile literature
   I. Title
   796.8'153   0431 110 425 4212

Acknowledgements
The Publishers would like to thank the following for permission to reproduce photographs:
Action Plus/R. Francis, p.5; Blitz, p.8; Silvio Dokov, p.29; Robert Harding, p.7. All other photographs by Trevor Clifford.

Cover photograph reproduced with permission of Sporting Images, Australia.

Our thanks to Sandra Beale, Director of Coaching, National Association of Karate and Martial Art Schools, for her comments in the preparation of this book.

Our thanks also to instructor Liam Keaveney and the students of Kokoro Karate Club.

Every effort has been made to contact copyright holders of any material reproduced in this book. Any omissions will be rectified in subsequent printings if notice is given to the Publisher.

Words appearing in the text in bold, **like this**, are explained in the Glossary.

CONTENTS

! Do remember that martial arts need to be taught by a qualified, registered instructor, or teacher. Don't try any of the techniques and movements in this book without such an instructor present.

WHAT IS KARATE?

Karate is a Japanese martial art which developed many years ago as a form of self-defence. The word 'karate' means 'empty hand', because it uses no weapons. Instead, the hands and feet are used to make powerful punches, strikes and kicks, as well as to block the opponent's attacks. Today, most attacking moves are pulled, or held back, so that the opponent is not actually hit, because this would be very painful and highly dangerous.

Karate is a very popular sport all over the world. Men and women of all ages can learn karate in clubs and take part in competitions. Karate teaches young people to focus their mind, and helps them to become self-confident. It makes them strong in mind and body. At the same time, it teaches **techniques** of self-defence and is a very energetic form of exercise.

All over the country there are many recognized karate clubs with experienced teachers.

WHERE TO LEARN AND PRACTISE

This book tells you how to set about starting karate. It also shows and explains some karate techniques, so that you can understand and practise them. But you must always remember that you cannot learn a martial art just from a book. To study and take up karate seriously you must go to regular lessons with a qualified teacher, so that you learn all the techniques properly and then repeat and practise them many times.

These figures are from an ancient Chinese temple. Karate was later developed from this style of fighting.

SHOKOTAN KARATE

When Funakoshi finally opened his own karate training centre, it was called *Shotokan*, or 'Shoto's club'. This became the name of his style of karate, which is still one of the most popular styles in the world.

After World War II ended in 1945, many American soldiers served in Japan. They took their knowledge of karate back to the USA and opened martial arts schools. Karate then spread to Europe and the rest of the world. It was not long before a world organization was formed to run karate as a sport.

KARATE WORLD CHAMPIONSHIPS

The first world championships were held in the Japanese capital, Tokyo, in 1970, and the first ever individual and team events were won by the Japanese. Ten years later weight categories were introduced for men, and the first women's event was staged – and won by a Japanese contestant.

Today, top competitors take part in world championships every two years. And just as importantly, boys and girls all over the world enjoy learning about and practising the fascinating art of karate.

EQUIPMENT

Karate is practised and performed in a special white outfit called a *karategi*, or gi (you say 'gee') for short. It is best to buy a gi through your club, but you don't need one immediately. For the first few sessions, a tracksuit or T-shirt and training bottoms will do.

The gi is all white. It is made up of a pair of trousers and a loose jacket tied at the waist with a belt. Girls wear a white T-shirt under the jacket. Gis are usually sold with a white belt, which is normally the right colour for a beginner. Make sure that your gi is large enough so that your movements are not restricted in any way. The trouser legs should not be dangerously long, although they will probably shrink when washed.

It is very important to treat your gi with respect. Always keep it clean. Wash and iron it regularly, and fold it carefully after each training session. A neat and tidy appearance shows that you have the right attitude to training. Inside the training hall, called a *dojo*, you must always have bare feet. A pair of flip-flops is useful to keep your feet clean as you walk from the changing room to the dojo.

PROTECTIVE EQUIPMENT

Some protective equipment is essential in case you or your opponent accidentally make contact. The most important are fist mitts, also called hand pads, and shin and instep pads. Groin protectors are a good idea for boys, and boys and girls should wear mouthguards in any form of competition.

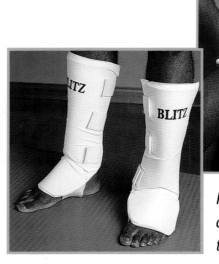

Fist mitts, and shin and instep pads, help to keep you safe.

PUTTING ON THE GI

1 Put the trousers on first. Many gi bottoms are elasticated at the waist. If they have a drawstring, pull it and tie it with a bow. Next put on the jacket, crossing the left side over the right side.

2 To tie the belt, pull it across your stomach first, keeping the two ends equal.

3 Cross the ends over at the back and bring them back to the front.

4 Cross the left end over the right, then pull it up behind both layers of the belt.

5 Finally, tie the free ends together right over left and pull them through to finish the knot.

 SAFETY

In order not to harm yourself or anyone else, don't wear a watch or any jewellery. Keep your fingernails and toenails trimmed short. Tie long hair back, but never with metal clips.

Make sure that you are fit enough to be very active, and don't train if you are ill. Exercise should not hurt, so never push yourself to the point where you feel pain. Tell your instructor if you suffer from any medical condition.

All martial arts can be dangerous if they are not performed properly. Never fool around inside or outside the training hall – or at home or in school – by showing off or pretending to have a real fight.

IN THE DOJO

It is important for any *karateka* (karate student) to show respect and **courtesy** to everyone and everything to do with karate, including the dojo, or training hall. Always bow to your instructor or to the **senior grade** karetakas when you go into the dojo. If there is no one in the dojo when you enter, stop inside the entrance and bow to the middle of the hall. Always do the same when you leave the hall.

THE STANDING BOW

You also make the standing bow before and after every exercise, and to an opponent before and after each contest. Put your heels together and place your hands flat against your thighs. Then bow smoothly by bending your upper body forwards, but not too far. Count to two as you hold that position. Always look at your opponent or whoever you are bowing to. Then straighten up again, move your feet apart and clench your fists.

Courtesy is a traditional and important part of karate. One way of showing courtesy is the standing bow.

THE KNEELING BOW

At the beginning of a training session all students perform a kneeling bow to the *sensei* (teacher). The senior grade will call '*Seiza!*' ('Kneel!'). Place your left knee on the floor, with your hands flat on your thighs. Then bring your right knee down, point your toes and sit back on your calves, keeping your back straight and looking forwards. When the senior grade calls '*Sensei ni rei!*' ('Bow to the teacher!'), the whole class performs the kneeling bow together.

All karate students perform the kneeling bow before training.

From the kneeling position, put your hands or fists down on the floor in front of you and bend your upper body into a low bow. Count to two and then return to an upright kneeling position.

When the senior grade calls '*Otagai ni rei!*' ('Bow to your classmates!'), do another kneeling bow to the other karatekas. At the call of '*Kiritsu!*' or '*Koritz!*' ('Stand up!'), lift your left knee, then your right, and return to a standing attention **stance**.

11

WARMING UP

Karate gives you a lot of hard, physical exercise. It is important to warm your body up and stretch your muscles before training, so that you do not injure yourself. At your club you will always start a session with some warm-up exercises. You might begin by walking or jogging on the spot for a couple of minutes, before doing some stretching exercises.

TRICEPS STRETCH

The triceps is the large muscle at the back of the upper arm.

1 Standing up straight, raise your right arm and touch your right shoulder with your fingertips.

2 Push your left hand gently against your right elbow.

3 Lower your fingers down your back as far as you can without hurting, and hold that position for a count of eight.

4 Repeat the stretch with your left arm raised.

ARM CIRCLES

1 Stand up straight with your feet a shoulder-width apart.

2 Stretch your arms out to the sides at shoulder level and then take them around in forward circles. Do ten circles, making them as large as you can.

3 Repeat the ten circles, this time backwards.

CALF STRETCH

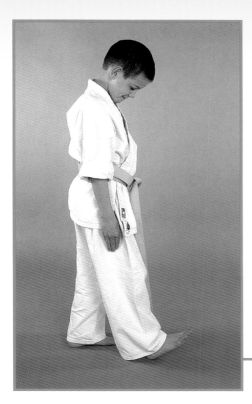

The calf muscle is at the back of your lower leg.

1 Stand up straight and put one foot about 30 centimetres ahead of the other.

2 Raise the toes of your forward foot as far as you can, keeping your heel firmly on the floor. Hold this position for a count of ten.

3 Repeat the stretch with the other leg.

! IMPORTANT

- Never exercise too hard when it is very hot or humid.

- Never exercise or practise karate when you are ill or injured.

- Try not to breathe too hard and fast when you are exercising or resting.

- Don't hold your breath while you are exercising or practising karate.

- When you are stretching, you should always remain comfortable and your muscles should not hurt. If you feel pain, stop at once.

- Begin your karate exercises immediately after warming up.

PUNCHING

In karate, your main weapon is the closed fist, which is used to punch. It is important to make a fist correctly, so that your punch is as powerful as possible but does not hurt you, the striker. Power comes from having the fist, wrist, elbow, shoulder and other parts of your body all acting together. You can practise this by punching a special pad held up by your opponent. Remember, when you punch in a **sparring session**, your fist must stop just short of your opponent so that he or she is not actually touched. Fist mitts are important in case you do accidentally strike your opponent (see page 8).

MAKING A FIST

1 To make a fist, first fold your fingers down. Then fold your thumb across the index and middle fingers, to lock them in.

2 In a karate punch you aim at the target with the first two knuckles. Keep your fist straight in line with your lower arm, so that the wrist does not bend when you hit the target. But make sure that your arm stays slightly bent at the elbow when you punch, so as not to put too much strain on your elbow.

Making a fist

! When making a fist, never put your thumb inside your fingers. If your thumb is on the inside it can be badly hurt, or even broken, when you punch.

PRACTISING THE BASIC PUNCH

1 Start in the attention **stance**, with your heels together and your palms on your thighs. Move into the ready stance by stepping to the side with the left foot, followed by the right foot. Make closed fists in front of you.

2 Move your feet further apart and bend your knees so that you are in the horse-riding stance. Push your right fist forwards, with the palm downwards. Then pull your left fist to your side, turning the palm upwards.

3 Pull your right fist back, and at the same time push your left fist forwards, so that your two fists pass each other in front of you.

4 Before your right arm reaches your body, turn it so that the palm is upwards. At the same time turn your left fist round into the punching position and make an imaginary punch.

5 Go back to the beginning and repeat the punch up to ten times. Then change over so that you punch with the right fist, and repeat this ten times.

KICKING

In karate, kicks are even more powerful weapons than punches. Kicks have a greater reach, but because they have to travel a long way to hit their target, an opponent has more time to avoid them. Most karate kicks begin with the leg bent at the knee. The leg is then straightened to hit the target with the foot, but never with the toes. It is important to keep the leg slightly bent, so as not to put too much strain on the knee.

There are four basic kicks – front, side, back and roundhouse.

FRONT KICK

1 You will probably learn this kick first. Start off in the ready **stance** (see page 15) and then slide your left foot forward. Bend your knees and keep your left fist up to guard your face.

2 Bring your right leg forward and raise your right foot, pulling the toes back.

3 When your right knee is high, thrust out your right leg, pushing your hips into the kick and keeping your toes pulled back. Imagine that you are hitting the target (your opponent's chest) with the ball of your foot – the hard area just behind the toes. Keep your guard up during the kick.

4 After the kick, pull your leg back quickly and put your foot down gently on the floor, in as controlled a way as possible. Do this after all these kicks.

SIDE KICK

1 With this kick, you hit the target with your heel and the little toe edge of the foot. Start with your legs apart and your knees bent, and hold your clenched fists at your thighs.

2 Lean to the left, away from the target, and raise your right knee across your body. Point the heel of your right foot directly at the target and then drive your leg out in a straight thrusting action. As you do this, it is important to lift your big toe and turn down the other toes on the kicking foot.

BACK KICK

1 This kick involves turning your back on your opponent, so you should only use it as a surprise move or after another attacking **technique**.

2 Keep your eyes on your opponent as you lift your right foot and thrust it back in a straight line, heel first.

ROUNDHOUSE KICK

1 With this kick, you can strike with either the instep or the ball of the foot, curling around into the side of the target. If you are very close, you can use your shin.

2 Point your toes as you bring your left knee up and across your body. Twist on your supporting leg and kick across the front of your body, straightening your ankle as much as possible and keeping your toes turned down.

BLOCKING

In any martial art, players have to learn to defend themselves against attacks by their opponent. Even the best attacking *karatekas* also need good defending **technique**. All the basic moves in karate start with a block, which is used to defend an attack by the opponent.

There are different types of block, including the knife and scooping block. Using blocks reminds the karateka that the true spirit of karate is never to strike the first blow but to defend against aggression. A good block will upset the opponent's balance and force them into a position where they are open to a **counter-attack**.

KNIFE BLOCK

This block protects the face and chest, using the little-finger edge of the hand to deflect (turn away) a punch or strike. The blocking hand is open and flat, with the fingers pressed together and thumb pressed into the side of the hand. This 'knife hand' is similar to the 'karate chop' that a lot of people associate with karate.

1 Take up the ready **stance**. Slide your right foot forwards and put your right arm up, with the palm facing forwards.

2 Step forwards with your left foot, drop your right arm so that your hand faces forwards, and bring your left hand to the right side of your face.

3 Draw your right hand back to your chest and face your left palm towards the blow coming from your opponent, keeping your left arm bent.

4 Block the strike with the outside of your left hand and push it away and down to the left, with a cutting action (which is why it is called a knife block).

SCOOPING BLOCK

This is a good defence against a front kick.

1 As your opponent lifts his foot to kick, twist your hips so that you turn sideways on. Bring your left hand around and under your opponent's ankle, deflecting the kick.

2 Your opponent is now off-balance, and you can punch with your right hand.

JAPANESE NUMBERS

In karate, counting is often done in Japanese:

		Sounds like:			Sounds like:
One	ichi	*ee-chee*	Six	roku	*rokoo*
Two	ni	*nee*	Seven	shichi	*she-chee*
Three	san	*san*	Eight	hachi	*ha-chee*
Four	shi	*she*	Nine	ku	*kee-oo*
Five	go	*go*	Ten	ju	*joo*

OMBINATIONS

Combination **techniques** link punching, kicking and blocking moves together in a series. This is when karate becomes more like a real contest. A defender might find it easy to block separate punches or kicks, but a series of them aimed at different parts of the body and coming from different angles is more difficult to defend against.

At first, you will follow combinations taught by your instructor. He or she will make sure that each individual technique is done correctly before the next one is added. As you become more experienced, you can add a greater number of more difficult techniques. Eventually, you will be able to make up your own combinations, using the techniques that suit you best. Practise them in front of a mirror to see if you are making any mistakes. It is a good idea to choose a different target for each technique, so that the defender has to keep finding different blocks. You must be able to use your combinations when you are advancing and attacking or retreating and defending.

FRONT KICK AND REVERSE PUNCH

This is a simple combination.

1 First front kick with your left leg (see page 16), and put it down in a forward position.

2 Then pull back your left arm and punch strongly with your right fist. This is called a reverse punch because the punching arm is on the same side as the back foot.

KATA

Kata means 'pattern' or 'form'. It is a series of set moves to improve technique and help a karateka learn about attack, defence and **counter-attack**. The moves are like training drills with an imaginary opponent.

At first each kata is practised in single moves, so that the student can learn and memorize each one. Then the moves are built up into a sequence, with a pause before each new one. Finally, the student performs the kata all the way through, imagining that they are reacting to an attacker or group of attackers. An experienced karateka flows through the complete drill, concentrating their attention, avoiding any hesitation and remaining balanced throughout the routine.

It will take many hours of practice before you reach this level. Then you will remember the sequences automatically and can concentrate on the imaginary contest.

This karateka is showing three moves from a kata.

SPARRING

Combination **techniques** lead on to the next aspect of
karate, called *kumite*, which means sparring. This tests the
skills you have learned and practised, on an opponent. At
first all the sparring is pre-arranged, which means that both
opponents agree beforehand what they are going to do.
This makes the contest much safer.

FIVE-STEP SPARRING

Five-step sparring (*gohon kumite*) is used to practise basic
attacks and blocks. Both karatekas know which attacks and
blocks will be used, so they can each concentrate fully on
their moves. After the fifth step, the two karatekas bow to
each other and change roles.

*These karatekas are practising their
moves during five-step sparring.*

KIAI

The *kiai* is a short, loud shout made at the end of any powerful
karate move. It sounds like 'Eee!' or 'Hai!', and it shows that your
mind and body are working together, in harmony. The kiai helps
to give power to your move, gives you confidence and scares your
opponent.

KUMITE SAFETY

When you are sparring with another karateka, you must concentrate very hard and make sure that you do not actually hit your opponent. Always work with your opponent, so that you help each other and learn together. The balance you learned during all those hours of practice will help you. Remember to look after yourself, too. Always keep your guard up, and take special care with your own head as well as your opponent's.

SEMI-FREE SPARRING

In this next stage of karate, both students know what sort of attack is going to be made, but the defender is allowed to choose his or her blocks and responses. For example, the attacker may be allowed to use only one kind of kick, such as the roundhouse kick. They can, however, change legs and aim at different parts of their opponent's body. The defender can use any blocking technique they wish.

Semi-free sparring is an important way of practising attacking and defending moves.

COOLING DOWN

It is important to cool down gently after energetic exercise such as karate. You can do this by jogging or walking, breathing deeply and by doing gentle stretching exercises like those you used to warm up (see pages 12–13). Some karatekas also like to cool down by doing some kata to music (see page 21).

GRADING

When you join a karate club, you are given a licence book and **insurance** against injury. You use the licence book to record your progress through the karate grades, called *kyu*. Each grade has a different coloured belt. You will probably start at the ninth kyu and you can then work your way up to first kyu, when you wear a brown belt.

This student is being given a licence book by her club.

BELT RANKS

Grades and belt colours vary between karate schools, but this is a typical system:

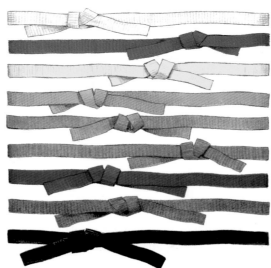

Belt colour		Kyu grade
white		10th or ungraded
red		9th
yellow		8th
orange		7th
green		6th
blue		5th
purple		4th
brown		3rd, 2nd and 1st
black		highest grade

At each grade there is a different set of karate **techniques** to learn, and to move up to the next grade you have to show that you have learned these completely. This is tested in a grading exam, which may be given by your instructor. You will have to perform basic karate techniques and certain katas, and also do some sparring. It is normal to have about 48 hours of training before you take each grading exam, so that there will be at least three months between each exam.

Grading exams test whether students are ready to move up to the next grade.

BROWN AND BLACK BELTS

A brown belt is a **senior grade**. It is made up of three kyu levels, third to first, which any karateka must progress through before aiming for the highest level of all, the black belt.

The black belt is split up into ten different *dans*, or degrees. The karateka must train for years between each dan, from first dan to the very highest, tenth dan. Very often promotion at this higher level is only awarded by a special panel of judges.

It usually takes four or five years for a karateka to gain a black belt, but this varies according to the rules of the karate club and may depend on how often he or she trains. Grades are important and are to be respected, but you will notice that expert karatekas show complete respect for lower grades and beginners. This is an important aspect of all the martial arts, and you should not worry too much about belt colours. Do your best to progress at your own pace, whatever age you are when you begin.

COMPETITION

There are many different opinions regarding competition in karate. Some people believe that sparring is the ultimate aim of all karatekas. Others think that personal development is more important. We take a look at the serious sport of karate on the following pages, but there are other forms of competition.

KATA COMPETITIONS

Your karate club or regional association may hold kata competitions. These are organized in age and grade categories. The katas are watched by a panel of judges, who give scores on a scale from 1 to 10. In some kata competitions there are three rounds.

FREE SPARRING

Karatekas are not allowed to try **free sparring**, in which the moves are not known beforehand, until they can perform all the basic **techniques** well and with confidence. Nothing is gained by sparring before you are ready, and obviously it could be dangerous. In addition, not all karate students like free sparring and prefer to stick to set routines.

Karatekas wait until they are confident with basic karate techniques before they try free sparring.

Sparring partners should be the same grade. It is always a good idea to wear fist mitts and other protective equipment for sparring (see page 8). You are not allowed to attack your opponent's shin, ankle, knee or groin, and you must take care not to hurt an opponent. If you ever feel that your opponent is losing control, step back, bow and go and sit cross-legged at the side of the dojo.

KUMITE COMPETITIONS

Some karate clubs concentrate on sparring, and spend a lot of time training for kumite competitions. These are held in age and grade categories, and sometimes in height or weight categories. Boys and girls compete separately.

In these competitions, points are awarded by judges for speed, accuracy and correct **technique**. A match is usually two minutes long, and the first person to score three points wins. Otherwise, at the end of the match the karateka with more points wins. There is an **arbitrator** and a set of referees for each match. To score a point, you must strike within 5 centimetres of the target area – head, chest and stomach – without the punch or kick being blocked. Referees can also award half-points.

The shaded areas are the target areas.

A WORLD SPORT

Karate is also an important international sport. In the world championships there are team and individual events in different weight categories, from super-lightweight to heavyweight. Senior men's competition is divided into seven weight categories, and senior women's into three categories.

CONTESTS

Karate contests take place on an 8-metre-square mat, with an extra safety area around it. Each match is controlled by a referee and a judge. They stand on the mat and move around it so that they always have a good view of the contest. A senior men's match lasts three minutes, and women's and junior matches last two minutes. The referee makes all final decisions, but he or she may ask the judge's opinion if necessary. An extra **arbitrator** sits outside the contest area, and he or she may also be asked to help in making a decision. A timekeeper and a scorer also sit outside the area.

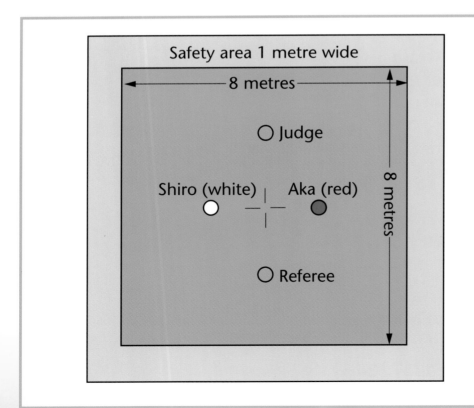

Safety area 1 metre wide

8 metres

8 metres

○ Judge

Shiro (white)   Aka (red)

○ Referee

This diagram shows the layout of a Karate match area.

THE POINTS SYSTEM

One of the two contestants wears a white belt and is referred to as *shiro* (Japanese for 'white'), and the other competitor wears a red belt and is called *aka* ('red'). To win the match, a contestant has to score three points. If neither does so, the one who has more points than their opponent wins. All points are scored by strikes to the opponent's target area. This includes the head and the upper body, but not the arms and tips of the shoulders. No contact to the throat or groin is allowed, and no physical contact is required for scoring. Light contact is allowed on the body, and only very light contact on the head.

The two contestants spar and exchange blows, blocks and **counter-attacks** until one of them achieves a strike. A full point (*ippon*) is awarded for a blow that is struck with good form, correct attitude, great vigour, alertness of mind, proper timing and from the correct distance. A half point (*waza-ari* or *wazari*) is awarded for a blow that is effective but not executed as well. Penalties are awarded for fouls and breaking the rules, which usually result in half a point or a point being given to the opponent. Too much physical contact always results in disqualification.

Karate is a very popular sport, with major world and national competitions.

JAPANESE WORDS

The Japanese words are pronounced as written here. When you see the letters 'ai', say them like the English word 'eye'.

Japanese words	Meaning	Japanese words	Meaning
aka, or *akai*	red	*Kyokushinkai*	way of ultimate truth
dan	degree		
dojo	training hall	*kyu*	grade
gohon kumite	five-step sparring	*otagai ni rei*	bow to your classmates
Gojo ryu	hard/soft school	*seiza*	kneel
		sensei	teacher
ippon	a full point	*sensei ni rei*	bow to the teacher
karategi	karate outfit		
karateka	karate student	*shiro*	white
kata	pattern, form	*Shito ryu*	Shito school
kiai	an explosive shout that gives power	*Shotokai*	Shoto's way
		Shotokan	Shoto's club
		Wado ryu	way of peace school
koritz	stand up		
kumite	sparring	*waza-ari* or *wazari*	a half point

GLOSSARY

arbitrator   senior referee who judges a karate contest

counter-attack   an attack that replies to an attack by an opponent

courtesy   polite, considerate behaviour

free sparring   practice contest between two karate students in which the moves are not known beforehand, so that the activity is 'free' or unplanned

pen-name   name a person uses that is not his or her real name

insurance   money paid in cases of injury

senior grade   experienced karate student who is at a high level or grade

sparring session   period of time when two karate students have a practice contest, sometimes with the moves agreed beforehand

stance   a position of the body, with the feet in a special place and the arms held in a special way

technique   a method you learn to perform a particular skill.

BOOKS

Junior Karate by Mike Pringle & Kingsley Johnson, Foulsham, Slough, 1997

Karate for Beginners by Pierre Blot, Sterling, New York, 1996

Karate for Kids by J. Allen Queen, Sterling, New York, 1994

Know the Game: Karate by David Mitchell, A & C Black, London, 1994

Play the Game: Karate by Karl Oldgate, Ward Lock, London, 1998

The Young Martial Arts Enthusiast by David Mitchell, Dorling Kindersley, London, 1997

Top Sport: Martial Arts by Bernie Blackall, Heinemann Library, Oxford, 1998

USEFUL ADDRESSES

UK Sport
40 Bernard Street
London WC1N 1ST
020 7841 9500
www.uksport.gov.uk

Sport England
16 Upper Woburn Place
London WC1H 0QP
020 7273 1500
www.english.sports.gov.uk

Sport Scotland
Caledonia House
South Gyle
Edinburgh EH12 9DQ
0131 317 7200
www.sportscotland.org.uk

Sport Council for Wales
Sophia Gardens
Cardiff CF1 9SW
029 2030 0500
www.sports-council-wales.co.uk

Martial Arts Development
 Commission
PO BOX 381
Erith DA8 1TF
01322 431440
www.madec.org

Sports Council for Northern Ireland
Upper Malone Road
Belfast BT9 5LA
028 9038 1222
www.sportni.org

World Karate Federation
149 Vizantiou St
14235 Athens, Greece
1 2717564
www.wkf.net

English Karate Governing Body
53 Windmill Balk Lane
Doncaster, N.Yorks DN6 7SF
www.ekgb.org.uk

National Association of Karate &
 Martial Art Schools
Rosecraig
Bullockstone Road
Herne Bay CT6 7NL
01227 370055
www.nakmas.org.uk

Australian Karate Federation
27 Sloane Street
Stafford Heights
Queensland 4053
07 3300 0022

INDEX

Titles in the *Get Going! Martial Arts* series include:

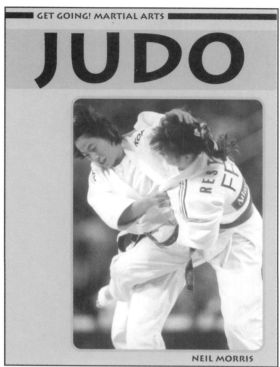

Hardback   0 431 11040 9

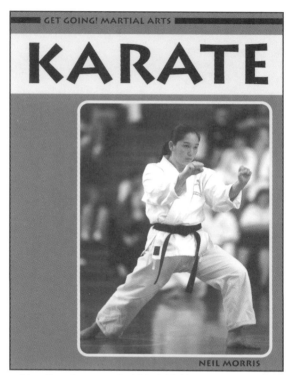

Hardback   0 431 11042 5

Hardback   0 431 11043 3

Hardback   0 431 11041 7

Find out about the other titles in this series on our website www.heinemann.co.uk/library